Allen Hinds

FUSION**BLUES** GUITAR**SOLOING**

Learn the Language & Creative Techniques of Modern Fusion-Blues With Allen Hinds

ALLEN**HINDS**

FUNDAMENTAL**CHANGES**

Allen Hinds: Fusion Blues Guitar Soloing

Learn the Language & Creative Techniques of Modern Fusion-Blues With Allen Hinds

ISBN: 978-1-78933-249-0

Published by **www.fundamental-changes.com**

For over 350 Free Guitar Lessons with Videos Check Out

www.fundamental-changes.com

Join our active Facebook community:

www.facebook.com/groups/fundamentalguitar

Tag us for a share on Instagram: **FundamentalChanges**

Cover Image Copyright: Author image, used by permission

Special thanks to Levi Clay for notation

Contents

About the Author...4

Introduction 5

Get the Audio 6

Chapter One – Three Essential Modes...7

Chapter Two – Building Solos with Motifs... 23

Chapter Three – Mastering Legato Technique 38

Chapter Four – Applying Legato Technique in a Solo 53

Chapter Five – Fusion Blues Vamp Soloing.. 63

Chapter Six – Bringing it All Together 73

Stay in Touch 87

About the Author

A native of Auburn, Alabama, Allen was exposed to Blues and RnB at an early age. Moving into Jazz and Fusion in his teens, he attended Berklee College of Music and, shortly after, moved to Los Angeles to attend Musician's Institute, where he was the winner of the Larry Carlton Scholarship. Allen joined the staff of M.I. where he teaches Jazz Improvisational Techniques.

Allen has five solo CDs to his name, and his sixth, *The Good Fight*, is shortly to be released. Besides his solo career, he has performed and/or recorded with Jazz and RnB luminaries including Hiroshima, Randy Crawford, Gino Vannelli, Patti Austin, Roberta Flack, BeBe and CeCe Winans, The Crusaders, Bobby Caldwell, James Ingram, Joan Baez, Boney James, Marc Antoine and many others.

Introduction

One of the things that first attracted me to the guitar, and continues to keep me exploring, is its capacity for creative expression. We fundamentally all play the same instrument, yet in the hands of players like B.B. King, Jeff Beck, Freddie King, Duane Allman, Derek Trucks and many more, it sounds totally different. The electric guitar especially, allows us to play one note and inject it with such emotion that it moves people.

There are tons of kids on YouTube these days who all have incredible technique, but there aren't so many who can really communicate a story with the guitar; one that is charged with emotion and grabs people's attention beyond flashy techniques. I'm not against technique – and it can be exciting to play fast some of the time – but often it's possible to say more by doing less and by making every note count.

Guitar students frequently ask me about my approach to soloing, because they're looking for strategies that will help them build better solos. In this book, I share some of my ideas for creating more engaging solos and pass on some exercises and tips to get you thinking more melodically.

All the best guitar solos we've ever heard are like stories. They have a beginning, a middle and an end; they have light and shade, dramatic and more reflective moments; they take us on a journey, and they communicate a range of emotions. We will look specifically at the topic of motif-based soloing, because it is one of the strongest "storytelling" devices available to us. As a mature player, you should be able to play something melodic that everyone can relate to. Remember that not everyone in your audience is a guitar head. Many people just enjoy music because they are moved by beautiful, emotive melodies, so be sure to give that to them!

I'll also explain how to develop the legato technique used extensively in my playing – as students constantly ask me about that – and show how to apply it in a musical context.

Throughout, we'll look at the vocabulary I use in major, minor and dominant contexts. There is plenty of contemporary fusion-blues language to learn, and you can practice these ideas by jamming over the backing tracks that come with the book.

I hope you enjoy it!

Allen

Get the Audio

The audio files for this book are available to download for free from **www.fundamental-changes.com.** The link is in the top right-hand corner. Click on the "Guitar" link then simply select this book title from the drop-down menu and follow the instructions to get the audio.

We recommend that you download the files directly to your computer, not to your tablet, and extract them there before adding them to your media library. You can then put them onto your tablet, iPod or burn them to CD. On the download page there are instructions and we also provide technical support via the contact form.

For over 350 free guitar lessons with videos check out:

www.fundamental-changes.com

Join our free Facebook Community of Cool Musicians

www.facebook.com/groups/fundamentalguitar

Tag us for a share on Instagram: **FundamentalChanges**

Chapter One – Three Essential Modes

Although there are numerous modal scales we could use for soloing – each of which would bring its own unique color and sound to a piece of music – in most real-life musical situations (especially in a fusion-blues context), there are just three that are essential to know and are used all the time.

These are the Ionian (Major scale), Dorian and Mixolydian modes. These basic major, minor and dominant sounds are where we'll spend the vast majority of our time when soloing. Other sounds, such as the Lydian, Phrygian, or the modes of the Melodic Minor scale, may crop up, but far less frequently.

Sometimes we reach for an altered scale because we're bored with playing the same old licks and are looking for something new to help us break out of a rut. But this can be because we've never fully mastered the three basic scales, and we've not learned how to apply them musically to their full potential.

Why think modally?

When we look at a piece of music, we can identify groups of chords that belong to a particular harmonic "family". For example, the familiar ii V I sequence (Dm7 – G7 – Cmaj7 in the key of C Major). Or, just the ii V cadence, Dm7 to G7, which suggests a C Major tonality.

We could solo over either sequence using only the C Major scale and we'd be playing all the right notes, but it could easily sound unfocused and unexciting. Thinking modally can help us to create more melodically sophisticated lines that move smoothly through the chord changes.

Thinking modally gives us a more colorful harmonic palette to work with. We could, for instance, choose to focus on the minor sound of the ii V and play the D Dorian scale. Or, we could go for a dominant sound and use the G Mixolydian scale. The modes are all about understanding a scale and using it musically, *in context*.

How we learn to play modal scales, however, is very important – because *how we learn* them will inevitably affect *how we apply them*.

Learning modal scales

There are various systems for learning scales on the guitar that are centered around specific zones on the neck. The CAGED system is one that is often used, or the interlocking patterns of the pentatonic scale, etc. While these approaches are great learning tools, and simple to engage with, the downside is that they often lead us to use repetitive shapes when soloing.

To achieve real freedom on the guitar, we really need to break away from small pattern thinking and be able to visualize any scale as one big pattern that covers the entire fretboard. If you can get to grips with this approach, eventually you'll find that you are able to jump into a scale at any point on the neck and know exactly where all the intervals are located – and you won't be constrained by jumping from position to position.

Here is an exercise I use with my students to help us move away from positional thinking and train our ears to hear the intervals in a scale anywhere on the neck. I'll demonstrate it with the D Major scale.

As basic as it sounds, the first step is to play the scale on one string. In Example 1a, play the D Major scale from the open fourth string and ascend the scale to the D note at the 12th fret. (Don't worry, things quickly become more interesting!)

Example 1a

Now play through the exercise again and this time take special note of the pattern of whole steps and half steps that form the scale. Listen carefully to the scale intervals and internalize their sound.

Now move over to the third string and play the D Major scale from the open G. Ascend the D Major scale and don't stop until you reach the D note at the 19th fret. This time, because you're beginning on a G note, the 4th degree of the scale, you'll need to let your ears guide you as you listen for each successive interval.

Example 1b

Now repeat the process on the second string. This time you're beginning on the 6th degree of the scale. Keep ascending the B string to the 15th fret.

Example 1c

Finally, jump over to the first string to complete the exercise. This time you're beginning on the 2nd/9th interval of the scale. Ascend the scale to the 22nd fret, or as high as you can go.

Example 1d

```
   ####4                                                                     2
  /  #  4
 (   #
  \        0----2----3----5----7----9----10---12   14---15---17---19---21---22
 T
 A
 B
```

For completeness, repeat this exercise on the fifth and sixth strings too.

The next step in the learning process is to take one of the single string scale patterns you just learned and work at being able to play the scale from any point *horizontally* across the strings. Here's how that works…

Let's use the first string as our jumping off point. Pick a note at random from the D Major scale, let's say the A note at the 5th fret. From that note, descend the D Major scale across the strings and try to keep roughly in the same zone of the neck (using the one-finger-per-fret rule). You should end on an F# note on the sixth string.

Example 1e

```
   ####4     1                              2                          3
  /  #  4
 (   #
  \        5----3----2
 T               5----3----2
 A                   4----2
 B                        5----4----2
                              5----4----2
                                   5----3----2
```

Let's try that again, this time beginning with the B note on the first string 7th fret. Descend the scale and you will end on an A note on the sixth string.

Example 1f

```
   ####4     1                              2                          3
  /  #  4
 (   #
  \        7----5
 T              8----7----5
 A                   7----6----4
 B                        7----5----4
                              7----5----4
                                   7----5----(5)
```

Now reverse the line you just played. Begin from the low A note and end on the high B.

Example 1g

Perhaps you already know the scale quite well beginning from a note on the first string, so this time let's start with the E note on the D string 2nd fret. Ascend the scale up to the A note on the first string 5th fret, then descend all the way down to the F# on the sixth string 2nd fret.

Example 1h

The major scale is a very familiar sound to us, so as you played these exercises you may have thought, "Oh yeah, this is how this shape relates to this major scale pattern that I already know."

But I don't want you to think about scale shapes, I want you to train your ears to *hear the intervals* of the scale. Rely on your ears more than your eyes and you'll begin to break down the barrier to playing freely on the guitar neck. If you can train yourself to hear what interval comes next, you'll eventually be able to play anywhere, and no part of the neck will be out of bounds.

Let's try this exercise with the D Dorian scale (D E F G A B C). Play a D minor chord, take a moment to internalize its sound, then play the D Dorian scale from the open B string. We're beginning on the 6th degree of the scale and ending on the 4th degree – the G note at the 20th fret.

Example 1i

As before, practice this idea from each open string – it will help you to internalize the sound of the scale intervals.

In due course, we can have some fun with this idea and sequence the notes. Here's a simple pattern that begins with the second available D Dorian scale note then takes one step back. The pattern repeats all the way up the neck.

Example 1j

This example begins on the open second string and ascends four scale notes. Then we slide back to play the second available scale note and ascend four notes again. The pattern repeats up the neck.

Example 1k

```
T---0--1--3--5--1--3--5--6---3--5--6--8--5--6--8--10---6--8--10--12--8--10--12--13---10--12--13--15--12--13--15--17---
A
B
```

```
T---13--15--17--18--15--17--18--20---
A
B
```

Now let's apply the same test as before. We'll choose a random scale note on the B string and descend/ascend the scale across the strings within a zone. Let's take the E note at the 5th fret. We'll descend to the G note on the sixth string 3rd fret, then ascend all the way up to the A note on the first string.

Example 1l

```
T---5--3-------------------------------------------------------------5--6--8--5--
A-------5--4--2-------------------------------------4--5--7----------
B-------------5--3--2-----------------2--3--5--7--------------
               5--3--2----------2--3--5
                     5--3--5
```

Now let's start from the A note on the second string 10th fret, descend to the B note on the sixth string, and ascend to the D note on the first string 10th fret. Try this on your own first and don't look at your strings – just use your ears to tell you the correct intervals to move to.

Don't cheat! Here's how it should sound.

Example 1m

```
T|--10-8--------------------|------------------|-----------------|-----------------7--8--10--|
A|-------10-9-7-------------|------------------|-----------------|---------8--10-------------|
B|--------------10-9-7------|--10-8-7----------|------7--9--10---|--10-------------------------|
 |                          |-----10-8-7-8-10--|--7-8-10---------|                           |
```

Let's try a slightly different way of using this idea. Beginning on a random D Dorian scale note on the first string, we'll descend the scale across the strings, but this time aim to end on the lowest available D note. Let's start on the G note on the first string 15th fret. This time we're not concerned with restricting ourselves to a zone and you can finger the scale any way that is comfortable for you. We'll end on the D note on the sixth string 10th fret, then ascend back to where we began.

Example 1n

```
T|--15-13-12-----------------|-------------|----------------|-----------------12-13-15--|
A|--------15-13-12-----------|--10-9-------|----------------|-----9--10-12-14-----------|
B|-----------14-12-----------|-----12-10-9-|------10-12-----|--12-----------------------|
 |-----------------12-10-----|--------12-10|--12-10-12-13----|                           |
 |-------------------------13|-------------|--------------   |                           |
```

```
T|--12--13--15----|
A|----------------|
B|----------------|
```

Now we're going to move down a scale tone on the first string and play this idea again, starting from the F note at the 13th fret but still landing on the D on the sixth string 10th fret.

Example 1o

Now play the same idea from the E on the first string 12th fret.

Example 1p

In your next practice session, keep working with this idea, descending the scale tones from the first string. As you move lower, aim for the D root note on the fifth string instead of the sixth.

For completeness, let's do this same exercise with the Mixolydian scale. To mix things up, let's work with Bb Mixolydian. The notes of the scale are Bb C D Eb F G Ab.

First, play the scale from the lowest available note on the first string.

Play a Bb7 chord, listen to its sound, then play the Bb Mixolydian scale from the F note at the 1st fret, to the Bb note at the 18th fret.

Example 1q

Now, let's jump over to the fourth string. The lowest available scale tone is the open D. Play a Bb7 chord then play the scale from the open string. Close your eyes for this one and just listen to the intervals to play each successive note. Keep going until you hit the Bb note on the 20th fret. Here's how it should sound.

Example 1r

Finally, let's test ourselves by picking a random scale note on the G string. Staying in one position as much as possible, descend across the strings to the lowest possible scale note and ascend to the highest possible scale note.

Let's begin from the D note at the 7th fret. Descend to the Bb note on the sixth string and ascend to the C note on the 1st string 8th fret.

Example 1s

Here's one final exercise. This time begin on the C note on the D string 10th fret and ascend to the Eb note on the first string 11th fret. Now descend all the way down to the Bb root of the scale on the sixth string 6th fret.

Example 1t

How did you find these exercises? I hope they tested your ears more than playing regular scale patterns. Your long-term goal is to be able to hear the intervals of a scale and instinctively know whether the next note is a whole step or a half step away, rather than relying on visual patterns. This way, you'll really internalize the music and it will lead more naturally to being able to play what you hear in your head. It's very difficult to do that if you're locked into playing patterns.

In addition, the work you've done here will help you later when we come to work on developing melodic motifs. Before we get to that, however, I want to show you a creative exercise you can use to get the most mileage out of any melodic idea you might play.

Applying licks modally

When we learn new licks, whether from a book or a recording, we often just learn the *shape* of the line, rather than the notes it contains. Knowing the notes is good, of course, but I suggest that the most useful approach is to understand the intervals that the notes create against the underlying chord.

In this exercise, we're going to take a lick played over a D minor chord and work out the modal scale degrees as they relate to the chord. Here's the lick:

Example 1u

Let's examine the intervals that this line creates when superimposed over a Dm7 chord. We'll break it down into groups of notes, splitting bar one in half, then dealing with bar two.

Bar one has two groups of four notes:

F E D C

B G A F

Bar two's notes are:

G E F D E

D Dorian is the scale that fits the Dm7 chord and below are the scale notes with the corresponding intervals underneath.

D	E	F	G	A	B	C
b3	2 / 9	b3	4	5	6	b7

On the audio track I played a standard Dm7 chord in tenth position. The grids below show the chord shape and the notes/intervals in contains.

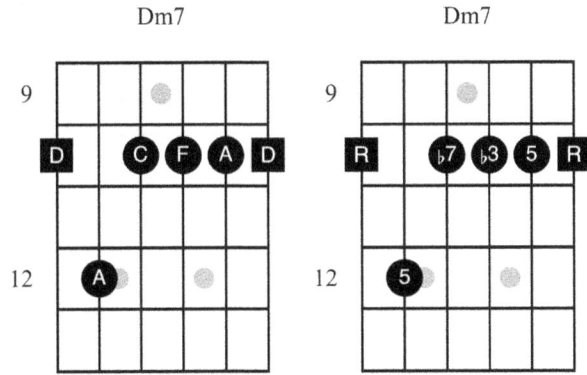

Here's the analysis of the groups of notes I played:

- In the first half of bar one, I played a b3 to 9th bend, followed by the root note, then the b7

- In the second half of bar one the B note is the 6th, which is followed by the 4th, 5th and b3

- Bar two begins with the 4th, then the 9th, b3 and root. The lick ends by returning to the 9th

Here's are Dm7 grids again, but this time I've superimposed the notes/intervals of D Dorian.

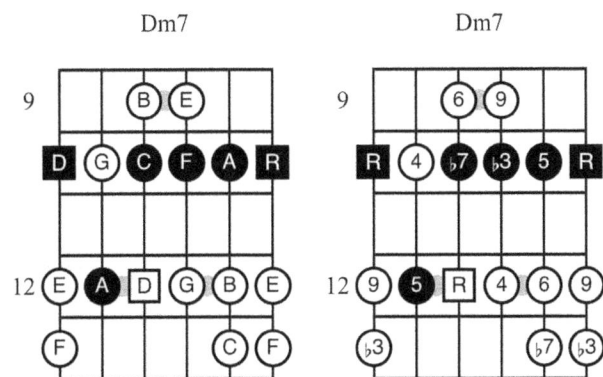

Pay special attention to the diagram that shows the intervals. If you can develop the skill of looking at a chord shape and visualizing not only where the defining chord tones are located, but also the adjacent scale intervals, you will quickly be able to compose licks that highlight specific intervals.

Referring to the diagram above and using the available adjacent notes we can, for example, play a line that highlights the 9th interval.

Example 1v

Or, we might choose to highlight the 6th.

Example 1w

It's also easy to visualize lines that move in intervallic patterns, like this one that highlights 4th intervals within the scale.

Example 1x

Work with this idea in your practice sessions. Take a familiar chord voicing and write your own grid for it. Note where the basic chord tones lie, and the other scale intervals are easily accessible nearby. Use the grid to write some licks that emphasize different intervals. This is an easy way to develop some vocabulary around a familiar chord shape.

Now let's take this idea a step further.

Modal analysis

Whenever I come up with a lick or grab one from a recording, I like to get maximum usage from it – I don't just save it for one context. So, why not see if the lick we played in Example 1u will work over other chords from the same parent key?

I improvised the line over a Dm7, which is chord ii in the key of C Major. Let's play the lick again, but this time over Cmaj7. Let's listen and hear how it works, then examine the intervals of the notes, now in relation to a Cmaj7 chord.

Example 1y

I think you'll agree that the line works well over Cmaj7, so let's consider the intervals we are now playing against the chord.

The C Major scale has the notes C D E F G A B and the formula 1 2 3 4 5 6 7

- In the first half of bar one, the lick begins with a 4th (F) to 3rd bend, followed by the 9th, then the root

- In the second half of bar one, we have the 7th, 5th, 6th and 4th scale intervals

- In bar two we begin on the 5th, followed by the 3rd, 4th, 9th and 3rd

So, what are we doing here? We're taking a lick and transposing it modally to alter its context. What's interesting about this approach is that, firstly, we can repurpose any lick we know to get more mileage from it. Secondly, we are more likely to invent licks we wouldn't normally think of when we transpose them.

When playing over a Cmaj7 chord, for instance, we might tend to begin a lick from the root, or perhaps the 3rd. How often would we choose to play a scale sequence that goes 4 3 9 R 7 5 6 4 as in bar one? But I think you'll agree it sounds pretty cool! And in bar two, the 3rd is a strong chord tone to end the line over the Cmaj7.

Let's try this over a couple more chords in the key of C Major. Here's the same line played over an Fmaj7 chord.

Example 1z

The appropriate mode for Fmaj7 in the key of C Major is the F Lydian scale.

F Lydian has the notes F G A B C D E and the formula 1 2 3 #4 5 6 7.

In the context of F Lydian, the scale sequence played in bar one becomes:

- Root, 7th, 6th, 5th, #4, 9th, 3rd and back to the root

- The phrase in bar two is 9th, 7th, Root, 6th and 7th

The notes worked out nicely to include the colorful #4 tone that highlights the characteristic Lydian sound.

Let's try another. Here is the line played over Bm7b5, chord vii in the key of C Major.

Example 1z1

The line still sounds good against this chord. Here, we are examining the intervals in the context of B Locrian, the appropriate scale for Bm7b5.

B Locrian has the notes B C D E F G A and the formula 1 b2 b3 4 b5 b6 b7.

- In the first half of bar one the lick begins on the b5 interval, followed by the 4th, b3 and b9

- In the second half we have the root, b6, b7 and b5

- In bar two, the intervals used are the b6, 4th, b5, b3 and 4th

Finally, let's play the lick over G7, chord V in the key of C Major, and examine it in light of G Mixolydian.

Example 1z2

This time, the scale sequence in bar one runs b7, 6th, 5th, 4th, 3rd, root, 9th and b7. In bar two we have root, 6th, b7, 5th and 6th. Again, it produces a cool sounding line.

Without getting too mind boggling, we can take this lick and "reverse engineer" the idea we explored earlier and seek out an appropriate chord voicing that it could be built around. The shape of the line suggests to me that it fits a G13.

Here's a G13 chord grid and the same shape with the adjacent G Mixolydian scale intervals.

You can now visualize how this lick is working against the G dominant chord.

Having worked through this process, we now have a single lick that will work over major 7, minor 7, dominant 7 and m7b5 chords.

To complete the picture, you can try it over the other two minor chords in the key of C Major: Em7 and Am7.

We have one lick for four different situations, but the important thing is to view it in the context of each tonal center. When you play a line, visualize it over different chord shapes, as we've done here, and work out what intervals you're playing over the chord.

This discipline will help you greatly when it comes to soloing over changes. If you can, for example, target the 3rd of each chord through a set of changes, playing that note on the downbeat each time, your lines will sound very secure and grounded. Then, knowing where the more colorful extended notes are located in relation to each chord shape will give you the option to create more interesting, less predictable lines.

To practice this idea, compose your own simple lick and audition it over every chord in its parent key. Then analyze the lick in the light of each chord, noting down the intervals you're playing.

Next, play a longer, more complex lick and repeat the process. I guarantee you'll soon be inspired and playing some new ideas.

In the chapters that follow, we'll explore how I apply the three essential modes in practical soloing situations. Parallel to that, I'll also show you some of the techniques I use to build interesting solos that (hopefully) tell a story.

Chapter Two – Building Solos with Motifs

Over many years of teaching at Musicians Institute Hollywood, one of the things I've noticed that students are consistently looking for is advice on how to build solos. *How do you play over changes? How do you build a good solo? What can I practice that will develop my ability to solo more melodically?* ...are questions that regularly come up.

We all have access to the same scales, of course, so it's how we use them that really differentiates us as musicians and causes some players to grab our attention more than others. In my opinion, the players who stand out are the ones who can take a simple idea and develop it. They begin with just a small seed of an idea, but they go on to tell a story with it.

Over the years, I've found that the advice that has most resonated with students is how to work on developing motifs, which is essentially a way of turning small ideas into big ones. That's what we'll address in this chapter through a set of exercises, then I'll show you lots of my motival vocabulary through a series of examples, culminating with a longer solo. This chapter is built around a tune that has a mostly Dorian vibe.

What is a motif?

To make it clear what we're talking about, a motif is generally defined as "a short musical phrase". The same could be said of a lick, but the difference between a *lick* and a *motif* is that the latter carries more significance in the overall composition – it's not just a throwaway idea.

A motif can be...

- A phrase that repeats at different points, like a musical hook

- An important recurring "theme" apart from the main melody

- A phrase that is stated then developed in various ways

- A melodic, rhythmic or harmonic cell

In practice, a motif is usually a phrase that we carry *through* a solo – a musical statement that we go on to develop, which gives our improvisation a sense of continuity.

There are numerous ways in which we can do this. We can...

- Adapt the phrase slightly to fit the next chord change

- Embellish it with passing notes

- Transpose it up/down the octave

- Play the same phrase, but over different chords

- Play different notes, but keep the same rhythm

- Keep the same notes, but alter the motif rhythmically

- Keep the same notes but displace the motif by beginning on different beats of the bar

It may not always be immediately obvious, but listen closely to solos by players like Eric Clapton, Jimi Hendrix, Robben Ford and Alan Holdsworth and you'll notice they all have one thing in common: they start simple and gradually draw their audience in, then build their solo (whether by complexity, intensity or both) as one idea leads to the next.

If you listen to a great lick in a solo, you eventually realize that the idea *came from somewhere*. In other words, it was informed by what was played before. That amazing lick isn't an isolated idea, it evolved from a collection of related ideas until it occurred naturally. This is one of the great benefits of motival playing – it gives you the space to develop an idea, to turn it around and look at it from different angles, and to keep expressing it until the magic happens.

Let's get started with some simple exercises that will instantly get you playing motifs. We'll take just four notes and play a phrase over a Dm7 chord. Here's my phrase:

Example 2a

When I'm sitting with a student, I'll usually prompt them to play the simple phrase and say, "OK, now find that motif and play it everywhere on the fretboard."

It's always interesting to me that we can play the simplest, throwaway lick, but then struggle to repeat it on different strings, or in different zones of the neck. It immediately tests our fretboard knowledge.

During your practice sessions, try playing a random lick, then work out how to play it *everywhere* on the neck. This will teach you a great deal about how the intervals of your lick fit together. You'll also notice that the same phrase sounds different in different zones, and especially when arranged on different strings.

Let's do this exercise with lick I just played. This is an easy one to accomplish; a more complex motif will test you a bit more.

Example 2b

To make things more musical, we can take this four-note idea and move it diatonically through a scale on one string. Let me explain how this process works.

We're playing over a Dm7 chord and I'm viewing it as chord ii in the key of C Major, so I'm aiming for a D Dorian sound.

The D Dorian scale has the notes: D E F G A B C

We're going to ascend the D Dorian scale on the third string (similar to how we practiced vertical scales on one string in the previous chapter) while repeating the motif. When we move to each successive note, we'll adapt our motif to stay within the notes of the scale.

However, we'll begin with the first note of our original random phrase: an A note on the third string 2nd fret. Then we'll move our motif to begin on the next scale tone: a B at the 4th fret. Then it'll be the C at the 5th, and so on.

Here's how this idea sounds:

Example 2c

I stopped when I arrived back at my original lick.

To create this example, I focused *only* on the scale tones on the third string. I then relied on my ears to tell me whether the other notes of each phrase were correct.

In reality, *every* note of the phrase ascends a scale tone each time, but that's too much information to think about and it's good ear training to narrow our focus.

I encourage you to come up with your own, similar phrase, right now to play over Dm7. Repeat the previous exercise using your phrase and move your motif diatonically, ascending the D Dorian scale on the third string.

Use *only your ears* to begin with. You know what your original phrase sounds like, so when you transpose it to the next scale step, just listen carefully to get all the right notes in the phrase.

There are no weird intervals in this scale, so you should be able to nail this idea pretty quickly.

Now, play a new phrase, and move this new motif diatonically through the scale.

It's really important that you work on developing this idea for yourself, because you're going to learn by the "doing" of it. You can probably already hear how taking a seed of an idea and transposing it through a scale has turned a small motif into a big motif. We've been able to compose a longer line that makes perfect musical sense and has some movement and direction.

In a nutshell, this is the essence of motif development.

To get the maximum mileage out of our original phrase, we can relocate the idea to a different three-string grouping and use a different string as our focal point. Let's arrange the motif on the fourth, third and second strings, and focus on ascending the D Dorian scale on the second string.

In order to keep playing the lick in exactly the same way, with a pull-off on the middle string of the group, we need to begin the motif on the C note located on the second string 1st fret. Then we'll move to the D note on the 3rd fret, and so on. Strum a Dm7 chord, then play through the following example.

Example 2d

This time, I kept the motif going until I ran out of frets.

Now, let's move the idea across onto the top three strings, and ascend the D Dorian scale on the first string, beginning with the lowest possible note that will enable the lick to be played the same way as before. It turns out that this is the open E string. Play through it now.

Example 2e

Again, I kept the idea going until I ran out of frets.

Let's review what we've achieved so far: we improvised a simple, four-note phrase. This was the starting point for our motif. Then we transposed that phrase through the parent scale of D Dorian. Next, we transferred the idea to two other string sets.

From that seed of an idea, we've covered the entire range of the neck on different strings, and we only played the idea ascending. We can follow the same process descending.

We could also play the motif faster, as a 1/16th note run. Alternatively, we might decide to play it slower, but break up the line by varying the note length between phrases and applying some rhythmic syncopation. The creative potential is huge, plus our line is super-musical because we're only using scale tones.

How about we try a slightly more complex phrase now?

This makes it a bit more of a challenge to move the motif through the scale and hear all the right notes, but it's good ear training. You're also learning the pattern of the scale all over the neck as you do it. Here's my next improvised phrase:

Example 2f

Beginning with this phrase, this time we'll descend the scale on the third string.

Example 2g

Now let's try a different descending motif that begins with the E note on the first string 12th fret. This idea creates a nice lick that cascades down the fretboard. You play pick every note or play it more legato like me, as you prefer.

Example 2h

```
1                                                    2
 3                         3                           3                    3
E|--12--13--12--10-----------------------------------|--10--12--10--8--------------------------------|
B|-----------------13--12--10------------------------|----------------12--10--8----------------------|
G|--------------------------12--10-------------------|--------------------------10--9----------------|

3                                                    4
 3                         3                           3                    3
E|--8--10--8--7--------------------------------------|--7--8--7--5-----------------------------------|
B|-----------10--8--6--------------------------------|-----------8--6--5-----------------------------|
G|--------------------9--7---------------------------|-----------------7--5--------------------------|

5                                                    6
 3                         3                           3                    3
E|--5--7--5--3---------------------------------------|--3--5--3--1-----------------------------------|
B|-----------6--5--3---------------------------------|-----------5--3--1-----------------------------|
G|--------------------5--4---------------------------|-----------------4--2--------------------------|
```

So far, we've focused on adding more notes to our motif, but we can go the opposite route and play a more minimalist intervallic pattern.

Here's an idea that ascends the D Dorian scale on the second string, beginning on the root at the 3rd fret. The motif is a four-note phrase. After each scale tone, the next note in the scale is played, but an octave lower. As this second note is only one scale step away from the first, it would sound quite dissonant if it were not for the octave displacement and the fact that we are skipping a string. The third note is then a 4th above the second note, and the first note we played is repeated to complete the phrase.

As we transpose this idea through the scale it creates a more angular, ambiguous sound.

Example 2i

I hope you can see the vast potential of this idea and are inspired to see what you can do with it. Work through these ideas in your practice sessions and focus on taking a small idea and turning it into a big one.

Approach your motif from all possible directions, locating it on different string sets and using the range of the neck. Once you've worked it out in different locations, try mixing and matching string sets to create new ideas.

Apply it in a solo

Next we're going to look at how I practically apply this idea to an improvised solo. Playing over an RnB flavor D Dorian track, I'll show you some of my musical vocabulary and demonstrate how I go about building a solo.

To keep things from sounding contrived, I improvised a solo with no forethought or planning, and combined some bluesy licks with motival ideas that were developed spontaneously. At the end of the chapter you have the entire solo notated, but I'll highlight and break down for you some of the motif ideas that emerged.

The backing track for this tune is provided in the audio download, so you can practice individual licks and attempt the whole solo, but you can also just jam along and invent your own ideas.

Example 2j shows the opening bars of the solo. In bar one I play a standard blues lick to kick things off. The motif idea begins in bar two and is very simple: to emphasize pairs of notes from the D Dorian scale and to descend in 6ths.

To disguise this idea, I've broken up the rhythm and added embellishment notes around the pattern, but if you stripped all of that away, you'd see the following 6ths descending: A and F, G and E, F and D, E and C, D and B. I break away from the pattern halfway through bar four, where I begin to set up the next idea.

Example 2j

The next example continues where the previous one left off and highlights bars 5-9. Here you'll see an ascending motif pattern with subtle variations on a theme. The core idea here is ascending D Dorian scale tones on the third string, beginning with the C note at the 5th fret on beat 1 of bar one.

I build a motival lick around each scale tone as the line ascends. You'll notice that I don't repeat the motif slavishly, following the exact same pattern of notes each time. Instead, I play variations on the theme as the notes fall naturally under my fingers, but you can still hear the main motif idea.

Towards the end of bar three I begin to break away from this idea and shorten the motif and this naturally transitions into a blues lick at the end.

Example 2k

The next line, drawn from bars 17-19, uses a three-note motif. This time the idea is to begin on any scale tone and ascend three notes. I'm not ascending D Dorian scale notes in order this time, instead I'm focusing on a specific zone of the neck and reaching for easily accessible scale tones.

The three-note phrases are a mixture of 3rds and stepwise scale notes. The opening three notes are 3rd intervals, the next three groupings of three notes are stepwise movements, then we have two more groups of 3rds. The final three-note phrase breaks the pattern.

This is an example of a *rhythmic motif*. I'm less concerned with sequencing the scale and more interested in creating a strong, repeating rhythmic figure. The rhythm is broken up by the 1/8th note rest in bar one, which means that the last note of the fourth phrase is displaced into bar two. The same kind of displacement occurs in bars 2-3 and makes the line more unpredictable.

Example 2l

Similar thinking is at work in Example 2m. For this example, I'm again using three-note phrases and allowing rests to displace them. You'll also notice that I gradually transition from the high to low strings, then back up to the second string for the final fast legato run.

There's nothing too difficult here until bar three, the latter half of which is a fast 1/32nd note run. The timing is tricky, so you may want to slow things right down and focus just on the run that begins after the 1/16th note rest.

You'll find this lick easy to finger, as the notes are all located around tenth position and fall very naturally under the fingers. Just listen carefully to the audio recording to nail the timing and try playing along with me.

Example 2m

Dm7

```
T--15-13-12----------------------------------------------------------------------------------------------
A-------------15-12---10-----------------------------------------------------------------------------
B------------------------------12-10-9--------10-14-12-----------------------------------------------
                                             10-14-12----9-12---10-------------------------8-12-10--
                                                                        7-10-8--------------------
                                                                                      8-12-10------
```

```
T----------------------------------10-13-12-10----12-10------10------------------------------------
A------------9-12-10----------12----------------12-------12-10----9-12-10-9----10-9----------9------
B---9-12-10-------------------------------------------------------------12--------12---12-10---12--
```

Example 2n is a cascading descending lick, similar to one of the earlier exercises and, again, I allow for some variations of the motif. Towards the end of bar two I alter the rhythm to shake things up and then begin to shorten the motif, no longer playing the full pattern, though you can still clearly hear the main descending idea.

Like the previous lick, this doesn't require any gymnastics to finger the scale shapes – the main challenge lies in nailing the rhythmic "interruptions" that break up the line to keep things fluid. Practice it slowly to begin with, and make sure you can play the whole thing cleanly before bringing it up to tempo.

Example 2n

Now have a listen to the full solo on the audio example and begin to work through it. If you find certain sections difficult, isolate those bars, and slow things right down until you have all the notes and position changes under your fingers. Don't forget you can practice this over the provided backing track.

Example 2o – Full Solo

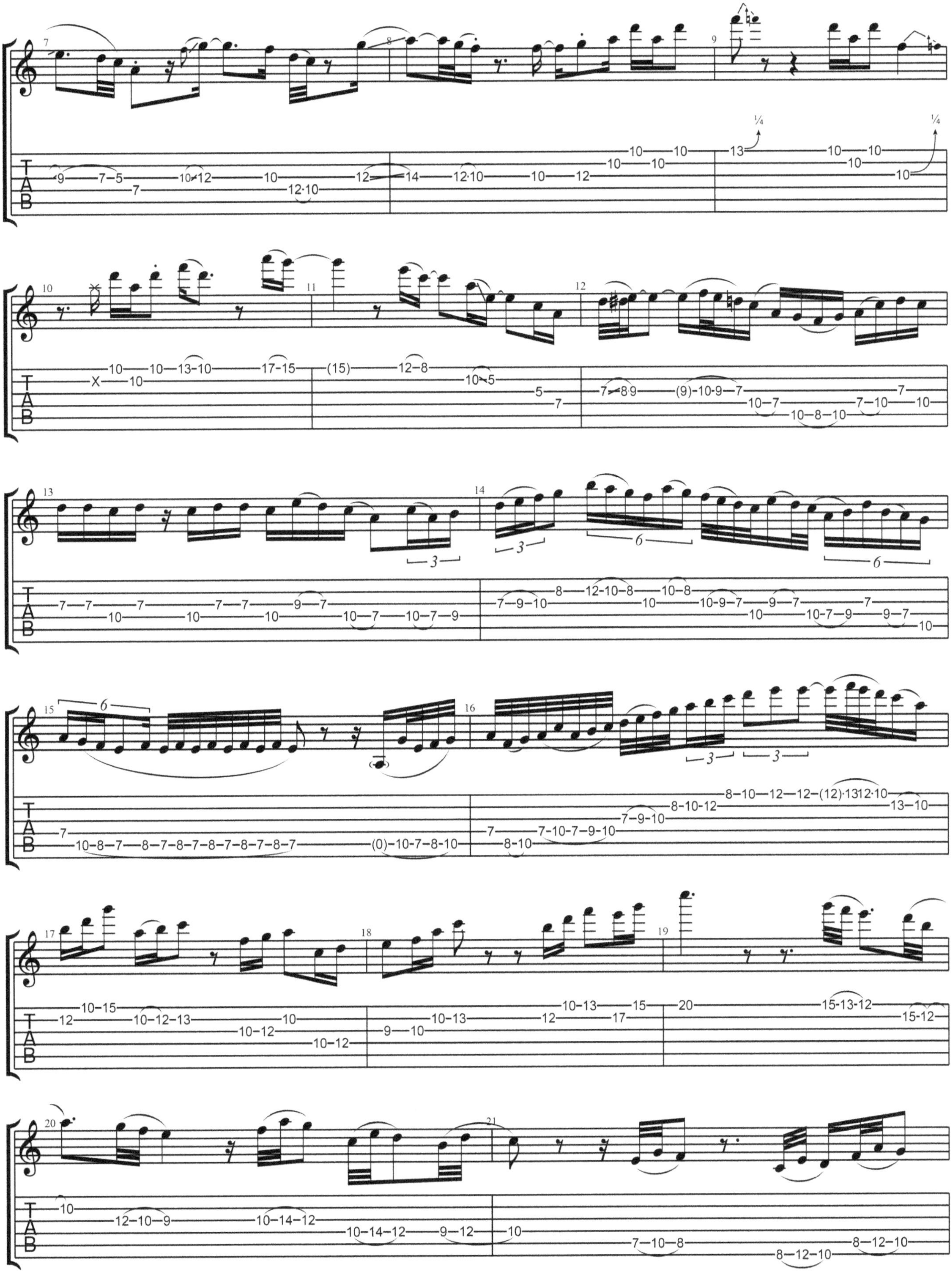

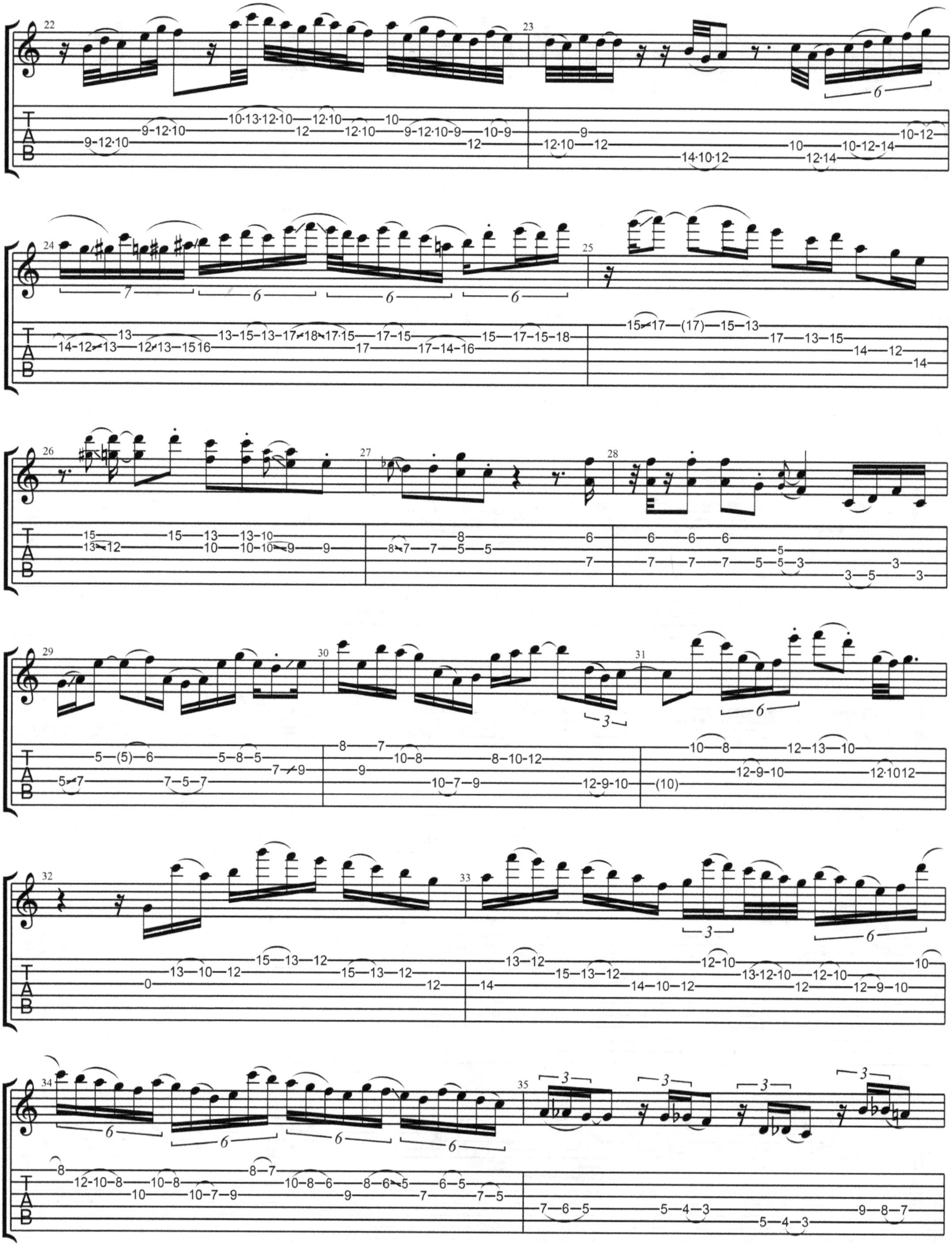

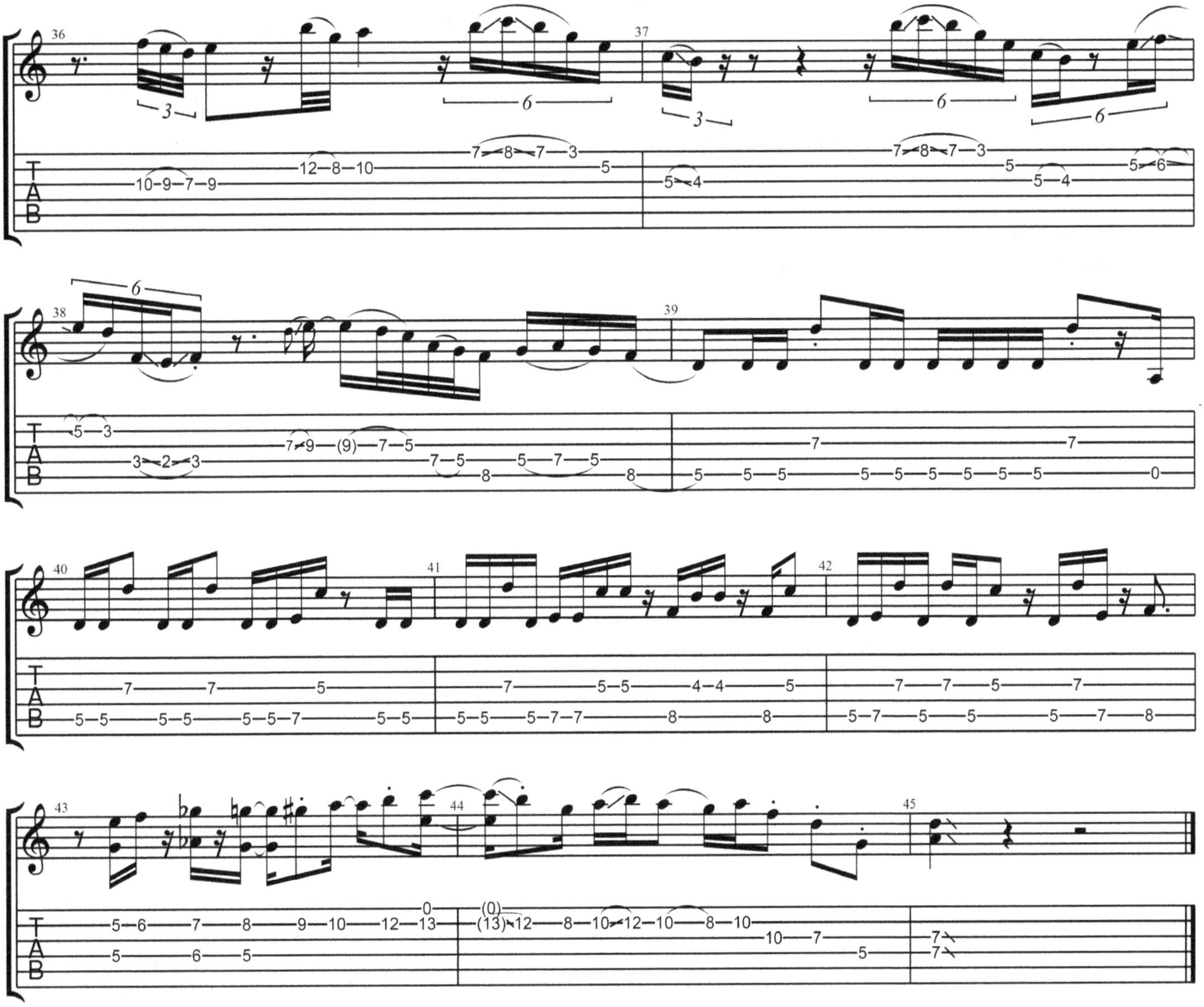

Chapter Three – Mastering Legato Technique

I'm often asked about my approach to legato technique on guitar and how I developed it. I've always found this a little funny – first, because for a long time I wasn't really aware that I had a legato approach, and second, because it arose due to my technical shortcomings. I just wasn't very good at alternate picking!

I hold the pick in a very unconventional manner, and despite different teachers trying to correct me over the years, I've given in and accepted that it works for me. There is no right or wrong way on the guitar, if it works for you and sounds good. Playing legato passages was my way of compensating for my picking technique, but over time I got good at it and it developed into a kind of signature style for me, which people recognize and appreciate in my playing.

Around the time I was developing my technique, I was influenced by different players who also made extensive use of legato, but none more so than Allan Holdsworth. I was immediately attracted to his fluid style and how he could play these long, flowing lines with wide intervals.

He sounded like no other guitar player and was an amazing innovator. I could see that he was using legato technique to achieve much of his complex harmonic vocabulary, so I focused on practicing that technique and applying it to my own ideas. The result was that I settled on a technique that combined a light picking hand attack (I almost brush the strings) and a strong fretting hand, which work together to produce a smooth legato sound. In this chapter I'm going to share a set of exercises that will help you to develop this approach for yourself.

Why use legato? Why not learn to alternate pick every note accurately and quickly?

It's a personal choice, of course, but for me, I find that legato allows phrases to breath. If you play a flowing legato run, it has much more dynamic range than a steadily alternate-picked run. Choosing to pick selected notes means you can make those specific notes pop out, and this brings more light and shade to your playing, and achieves a more saxophone-like effect.

I combine my legato approach with a vibrato technique I learned from Scott Henderson. Scott showed me how to "squeeze" notes and move them backward and forward horizontally on the fretboard i.e. pushing/pulling them from fret to fret, much like violin vibrato technique. Put these two techniques together and people say they can tell when it's me playing after only a couple of notes.

Legato is not for everyone, but hey, this is my book! Even if you don't go after legato style wholesale, you may find it useful some of the time and it will bring a contrast to your approach. So, read on and I'll share some tips for getting the best out of this technique in your playing.

In one sense, there's no real mystery to legato technique. It involves picking one note in a sequence and executing the rest using hammer-ons if you're ascending or pull-offs if you're descending. The trick is getting the notes to sound even, and for that we need some fretting hand strength, which we can develop through the following set of exercises.

Strengthening the fretting hand

When I was studying at Berklee, a common exercise students would practice is the one-finger-per-string chromatic pattern that is mirrored on each string. It serves no harmonic purpose but is useful for practicing alternate picking accuracy.

We can use that same exercise to practice legato technique and build strength in the fretting hand. In this first exercise, you'll ascend from the A note on the sixth string 5th fret, to C on the first string 8th fret. Lightly pick *only* the first note on each string and hammer on the rest. Go reasonably slowly, allowing time for each note to sound as much as possible.

Example 3a

Now try this in reverse using pull-offs from the first string C note, down to the sixth string low A. Once again, just pick the first note on each string. It's normally harder to make the notes sound clearly using pull-offs, so persist with this exercise. Picking fairly lightly is important, so that you don't have a first note that is much louder than all the others.

Example 3b

Now let's play a phrase that requires both hammer-ons and pull-offs, and also moves chromatically up the fretboard on one string.

Begin on the A note on the sixth string 5th fret, as before, and hammer-on chromatically up to C. This time, however, pull off from the C back down to A. This means playing seven notes legato from a single pick stroke. When you arrive back at the 5th, move up a half step and repeat the pattern from the 6th fret, and so on. There are no rests in between phrases, so this line just snakes up the fretboard, crossing the bar lines.

This is a great exercise for developing fretting hand strength. Remember that the goal is good note production – sounding each one as clearly as possible.

Example 3c

We can mix up this idea and approach it in many different ways. For instance, we can go back to playing horizontally across the fretboard and move the whole pattern chromatically.

Here we play horizontally from the sixth string 5th fret to the first string 8th fret, then shift up a half step to play the pattern descending from the first string 9th fret. When we arrive back on the sixth string, the pattern shifts up a half step again. You can keep this idea going until you run out of frets.

Example 3d

When moving positions, I'll usually do so using a slide. As you get deeper into legato and refine your technique, you'll find that executing a slide often gives you enough momentum to play the next legato phrase without needing to pick the strings, and this creates the fluid sound we're looking for.

In this next exercise, pick the third string to begin the descent, then the fourth string, pulling off from 7th to 4th fret. Then slide the first finger up from 4th to 5th fret and hammer on chromatically up to the 8th fret. You should now be playing eight notes on the fourth string but executing them all with a single pick stroke! Move across to the third string and play the ascending hammer-on to complete the pattern.

Restart the pattern on the third string a half step higher, as shown in bar two below, and continue for as long as you want.

Example 3e

At this point, be mindful of any fatigue building in your fretting hand. If you feel tiredness or tension beginning to set in, take a break and rest.

It takes time to build up strength in the fretting hand – it won't happen overnight. If you spend a little time every practice session doing your legato drills, gradually you'll begin to build the strength you need to make the notes sound fluid and even – but pace yourself.

Remember that, with all these exercises, the goal is to go slowly and achieve good note separation. It's about developing clarity rather than speed. Once you've fine-tuned your core technique, the speed will come. The better you get at legato, the more you'll hear each note distinctly, and the volume of non-picked notes will increase.

Practicing basic scales

Another good exercise is to practice basic scales using legato and we'll do that with the major scale.

When I play something like this, I don't have a prescriptive system that dictates which notes I pick and which I hammer on/pull off. In time, you'll find that your picking is there to support any phrase you play *as needed*. In other words, play as many notes as you can legato, but pick if your line is running out of steam.

That said, most of the time it will feel natural to pick whenever you have to change strings, and this is a good starting point for you to practice the technique. Here's the A Major scale played legato. Pick only on the string changes and just once per string.

Example 3f

To work on further strengthening the fretting hand, you can practice the last exercise by picking only the first note of the scale (whether ascending or descending) and hammering on or pulling off every other note. Of course, the notes do die off, but keep them going as long as you can.

Practice this plugged into an amp, so you can really hear how well you're doing it. If you have a good quality compressor pedal, that will help to smooth out the sound a little and get the notes sounding more even, but only apply light compression – it's not there to cover up bad technique.

If you prefer three-note-per-string patterns for your scales, then practice this major scale pattern ascending and descending.

Example 3g

To make things more interesting, we can start to work with scale patterns that use backtracking or sequencing. Here we are still following the principle of picking on every string change. Where there are multiple notes on one string (like the fifth string in bar one), these are played legato with a single pick stroke at the beginning of the sequence.

Example 3h

You can have lots of fun with this idea. Here's a sequenced major scale line that begins on the 5th (E) and ends on the A root. What's tricky here is that it descends five notes of the scale then six, and alternates between groups of five and six throughout to create a cascading effect.

Example 3i

While you're practicing these drills, you can also try abandoning the pick for a while and use the picking hand fingers to "assist".

I use my thumb for downstrokes and my first finger to pluck upwards. This gives the sound a contrasting attack, which I quite like. You can switch to using fingers only for quieter, more emotional passages of music, and back to the pick for louder passages.

The next example uses the C Major scale in a vertical pattern that uses more of the range of the neck and incorporates slides to move position.

Beginning at the 3rd fret, you'll play two notes on the fifth string. Next you'll play four notes on the fourth string, sliding from 5th to 7th fret with your fourth finger.

Next comes three notes on the third string, followed by four notes on both the second and first strings, each with a fourth finger position slide.

At the top of the run on the first string, slide your fourth finger from 10th to 12th fret and back to execute the changeover from ascent to descent. All seven notes are played with a single pick stroke.

Played over a Cmaj7 chord, this is a neat way to cover a wide range of the neck with a single legato run.

Example 3j

Practicing legato phrases

Now let's move on to practice legato with some musical phrases. Here's a drill that I've shown to many students over the years and takes some effort to get sounding smooth. It uses just three notes, whole step intervals apart, and requires a little stretch.

All the notes are on the third string and you'll pick only the starting note, an E at the 9th fret, fretted with the fourth finger. Pull off to the C on the 5th fret, hammer on to the 7th fret with the second finger, then hammer on at the 9th with the fourth finger. To complete the phrase, hammer on to the 7th fret with the second finger again, then pull off to the 5th.

Have a listen to the audio file to hear how it sounds.

Example 3k

I've only repeated it twice in the above example, but this is an ideal phrase to endlessly loop around. Drill it as many times as you can, picking just once at the beginning of each six-note sequence. It's easy to begin to play this one real fast and cover up any dubious technique, so don't do that! The harder but better option is to play it slow and really focus on nailing the note separation, achieving evenness of tone and volume.

Move this idea around the neck and play it in different zones on different strings. Here's how you can use it to create a cool phrase that works over an Em7 chord by playing it in the same place on adjacent strings.

Example 3l

You can also use string skipping to keep things interesting and challenge your accuracy.

Example 3m

Building legato licks

Of course, we can vary the legato pattern itself and choose a different template for our ideas, and we can also begin to develop melodic ideas that sound more like licks.

Here's an idea that starts in a similar way to our original legato pattern but varies it slightly and spills onto two adjacent strings. This is a C Ionian idea played over a Cmaj7 chord.

Example 3n

Don't forget that you can repurpose any lick by playing it over other chords that belong to the same parent key. In the key of C Major, this lick will work well over Dm7, Em7, Fmaj7 or G7.

Or how about Bm7b5 resolving to Cmaj7, as in the example below?

Example 3o

In the next example, I play another simple legato pattern that spans three strings. You can take an uncomplicated idea like this and arrange it so that it climbs up the fretboard.

Much like we did when discussing how to build motifs, this line ascends the D Dorian scale on the third string, starting from the A note at the 2nd fret. The line ends on a B note, implying a Dm6 sound. This line also sounds great over a G7 chord.

Example 3p

Dm6

Here's an ascending idea that works over an Fmaj7 chord and is built from an eight-note legato pattern. It's possible to play the eight-note pattern in such a way that you don't need to move position, but I've arranged it deliberately so that it calls for legato hammer-ons, pull-offs and position slides.

This approach turns a potentially boring phrase into a much more exciting melodic idea that has some momentum. Whenever you come up with a lick that you like, think legato. Can it be rearranged to take advantage of legato technique, including hammer-ons, pull-offs and position slides?

Example 3q

Fmaj7

Here's another example of how you can take a legato phrase and develop it into a motif, moving it through a scale. This idea is played over a Dmaj9 chord. This legato pattern involves a string skip, so let's look at it in isolation to begin with. Here it is played twice at a medium tempo.

Example 3r

Dmaj9

Now let's apply this pattern as we descend through the D Major scale. If you've been practicing your motif development, have a go at solving this puzzle using just your ears and listen for the next correct scale interval. If you get lost, here's the answer!

Example 3s

Some of my legato licks involve stretches, and I like the idea of being able to double up notes on adjacent strings if possible because it creates an interesting effect. Here's a pattern that I often teach students to help them develop this idea. It's a simple four-note pattern and here we're playing it using the A Dorian scale.

Fret the C on the B string 1st fret with your first finger, then execute a pull-off from the 5th fret with your fourth finger. Hammer onto the 3rd fret with your second finger, then play the F# on the high E string with your first finger.

Here's the basic phrase, played twice.

Example 3t

Am7

```
T  --5----------1----------3----------2----------|--5----------1----------3----------2----------|
A  ---------------------------------------------|---------------------------------------------|
B  ---------------------------------------------|---------------------------------------------|
```

Now we use that phrase to ascend the fretboard. We ended with an F# note on the first string, and we'll "almost" double it up by beginning the next phrase on an F# on the second string. Each time the phrase is played, the final note is the first note of the next phrase.

When I double up the F# note, I can manage the six-fret stretch to sound the notes almost simultaneously, but if you can't make the stretch, don't worry, just quickly jump position to play the F# on the second string with your fourth finger.

Here's how the pattern sounds ascending the fretboard. The lick ends with the same phrase it began with.

Example 3u

Am7

```
T  --5----1----3----2----7----3----5----3----|--8----5----7----5----10----7----8----7----|
A  -----------------------------------------|------------------------------------------|
B  -----------------------------------------|------------------------------------------|
```

```
T  --12----8----10----8----13----10----12----10----|--15----12----13----12----17----13----15----14----|
A  -----------------------------------------------|------------------------------------------------|
B  -----------------------------------------------|------------------------------------------------|
```

You can get the most out of this idea by transferring it to other strings. Try playing it on the third string, beginning with the phrase below, and use your ears to transpose it up through the A Dorian scale.

Example 3v

Now try it on the fourth string. Locate the lowest point on the neck where you can play the phrase, then transpose it upward through the scale on your own.

Staying in A Minor, here's a descending legato pattern for you to try. It's a six-note phrase that spans the bar line and involves quick fretting hand position changes to prepare for every subsequent phrase. Play through it slowly to nail the position shifts, then gradually bring it up to speed.

Example 3w

Finally, let's take this core legato idea and develop it further on the adjacent strings. You could approach this in any number of ways to make a more complex pattern – this is just one way. Here is the new phrase, which we've effectively doubled up.

Example 3x

Now, here is the phrase descending through the A Dorian scale. The result is a long line that cascades down the neck.

Example 3y

The line ends on a D note and suggests an Am11 sound.

In your next practice session, invent your own legato phrase and work at transposing it through a scale. Next, transfer it onto other strings, so that you can play it in different zones on the fretboard. This is a great way of honing your legato technique while simultaneously practicing motif ideas.

In the next chapter, you'll learn how I apply my legato vocabulary in a real musical situation.

Chapter Four – Applying Legato Technique in a Solo

In this chapter we're going to apply legato technique while soloing over a D Major blues. Here you'll learn how I apply Ionian (major scale) ideas in the context of a rocky blues track, which I tend to punctuate with D Minor Pentatonic ideas to create some variety in the vocabulary. Here, you'll see how I go about applying legato technique in a real musical context.

At the end of the chapter there is an improvised 24-bar solo for you to check out, but first we'll look at a few example licks.

There is some challenging material for you to engage with here, because I naturally tend to combine odd note groupings in my lines. The slippery nature of legato lends itself to the idea of floating across bar lines. I also find that when playing legato it's easier to combine odd note groupings than it is when you're alternate picking them.

When learning these licks, I advise you to slow them down to begin with. First make sure you have the fingering of the legato runs under control, so you can play them fluidly. Second, pay attention to the rhythmic phrasing. Listen a few times to the audio examples before attempting them.

The examples that follow can be grouped together in threes if you want to turn them into short solos. Examples 4a to 4c form a complete 12-bar pattern and the lines are constructed to flow into one another. Then examples 4d to 4f form the next twelve bars, etc. Let's get started…

* * *

Example 4a is one of the most difficult lines in this chapter, but we're going to tackle it head on. From here, everything gets a little easier! Listen to the audio track several times before attempting it.

The opening phrase is a standard bluesy lick, then we have a long legato line that begins near the end of bar one and continues into the first part of bar three.

This is a great example of how a legato phrase can defy the bar lines. Think of the open fifth string as the launchpad for this line, then treat the three groups of four 1/32nd notes that follow as the first part of the phrase. That gets us to the end of beat 1 in bar two. The notes choices all come from D Ionian, apart from the C note which is borrowed from D Minor Pentatonic.

I play the first group of 1/32nd notes with my first finger on the 3rd fret, second finger on the 5th, and fourth finger on the 7th. I'm comfortable with that stretch, but if you feel any tension in your hand, use your third finger to fret at the 5th. Also, tilt your wrist slightly into your body and you'll find your thumb naturally sits lower on the back of the neck and your fingers are better aligned with the fretboard.

Beginning on the second beat of bar two, treat the next six notes as the second part of the phrase, but look out for the rhythmic timing, which has the effect of creating a brief "pause" in the line. Here you'll need to make a position shift with the fretting hand. After playing the third string 7th fret with your fourth finger, quickly slide up to play that note again with your first finger.

Beats three and four of bar two have a six- and five-note phrase respectively, each beginning on the beat. After the fast 1/32nd note ascending run, the line begins to descend, and you can hear that the unusual mix of note groupings have the effect of pulling against the tempo.

In bar three, the line begins to ascend again, and in bar four I basically go nuts and speed up! Here I'm not thinking so much about the parent scale notes, I'm just working towards a target end note (the G on the first string 15th fret). In each group of notes, I'm playing a similar phrase that includes chromatic tones. Sometimes I'll just go for a shape on the fretboard, move the idea around and analyze what happened later. As long as you have a destination in mind, it's fine to experiment like this.

Example 4a

Example 4b begins with a short off beat four-note per-string phrase played entirely on the first string. In bar two we have a rhythmically syncopated motif constructed from 1/16th note triplets but grouped into fours *a la* Eric Johnson. Play close attention to the audio to get the exact phrasing used here. The line concludes in bar four with a 1/16th note pattern playing the same note (D) doubled across two adjacent strings and employing a quick finger slide.

Example 4b

This next lick is a Country-inspired line beginning with a series of soulful strings bends – a whole step, followed by two half steps. Bar two introduces a 1/16th note triplet line with a series of fast legato hammer-ons and pull-offs, typical of guitarists such as Brent Mason and Albert Lee. In bar three, there are some Jeff Beck style natural harmonics played entirely on the sixth string. The lick concludes with a sliding 1/16th note phrase in bar four.

Example 4c

The next example also uses 1/16th note syncopation and displacement to create rhythmic tension against the backing. The melody here hints at a Thelonious Monk tune. Take your time to note carefully where each phrase is placed against the beat and how it moves across the bar line between bars one and two.

In bars 3-4 the change from straight 1/16th notes to 1/16th note triplets creates the impression of the line speeding up, especially when they are grouped in sevens in bar four. Bars three and four are both played on adjacent strings so that a minor 2nd dissonance is heard between notes.

Example 4d

After a classic rock-style intro bend on the second string, large interval jumps spread across four strings take over at the beginning of beat four in the first bar and are carried across the bar line into the second measure. Using large intervals like this helps to create contrast and tension within a solo. After a more typical rock blues line in bar three, the lick ends with more diatonic seconds in the final bar to create some very effective dissonance against the harmony.

Example 4e

This lick begins on the V chord of the underlying progression with a series of Country-style 1/16th notes played entirely on the top two strings. Bar 2 again utilizes different note groupings, ranging from 1/16th notes grouped into five and regular 1/16th note triplets. Look out for the raked arpeggio on beat 3 of bar three. The line finishes with some off beat 1/16th notes to break up and contrast with the energy of the previous bars.

Example 4f

Example 4g begins with a type of enclosure lick – a common jazz and fusion embellishment technique – where the idea is to target the 5th (A) of the D major chord with passing notes above and below. From there, the idea was to create a moving motif filled with 2nd intervals, which is most noticeable in the final two bars. Bar four uses sliding minor 2nd double-stops to create some strong, effective dissonance against the harmony.

Example 4g

Although this next lick looks rhythmically complex, it's mostly 1/16th note triplets. Listen to the audio several times to get the sound of the legato phrasing in your head, then work on your fingering to take account of the string changes. After the long legato run, bar four concludes with bluesy trills to provide some melodic contrast.

To learn this lick I suggest breaking it down one bar at a time. Learn bar one, then bar two, then put them together. Then work on bar three and add it to the first two. Even break the bars in half if you need to.

Example 4h

There's a hint of my friend Robben Ford's phrasing in Example 4i, with the use of half step bends and large string slides across the bar line, such as at the end of bar one. Like several of the examples above, bars 1-2 are played exclusively on the top two strings before shifting across to the third and fourth strings.

In bar three, I used off beat rhythms to provide contrast to the run of 1/16th notes in the previous bar. This lick may require listening to the accompanying audio track a few times to really get the placement of each section against the beat.

Example 4i

To round off this chapter here is a longer 24-bar solo that demonstrates many of the techniques and approaches discussed in the examples above.

It's important to open a solo with a strong statement, so here we kick off with a rapid intervallic rock phrase. Use plenty of vibrato and you should be able to get this sounding a bit like slide guitar.

In bars 7-8, notice that the legato phrasing is punctuated by repeated hammer-ons and pull-offs to open strings (like those seen in Example 4c). These continue until bar eleven when a series of octave bends are introduced.

In bars 11-14, I went for a series of bends to give the solo some vocal-like phrasing. They are nearly all full whole step bends, apart from one blues curl, so make sure to focus on accurately bending to pitch.

Bars 15-16 have another 1/16th note triplet legato run. The final two bars build to a climax with some rapid-fire 1/16th note legato lines.

Example 4j

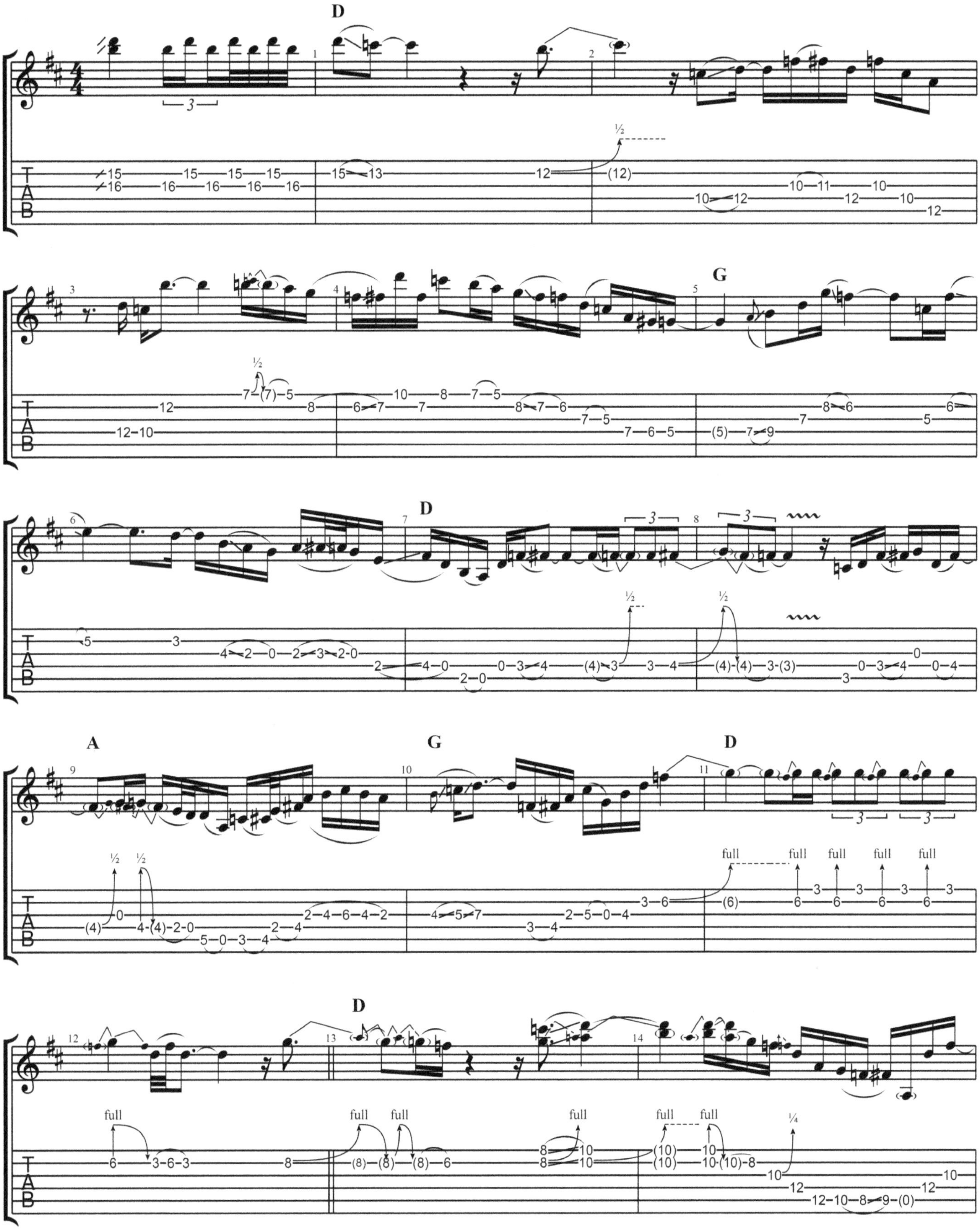

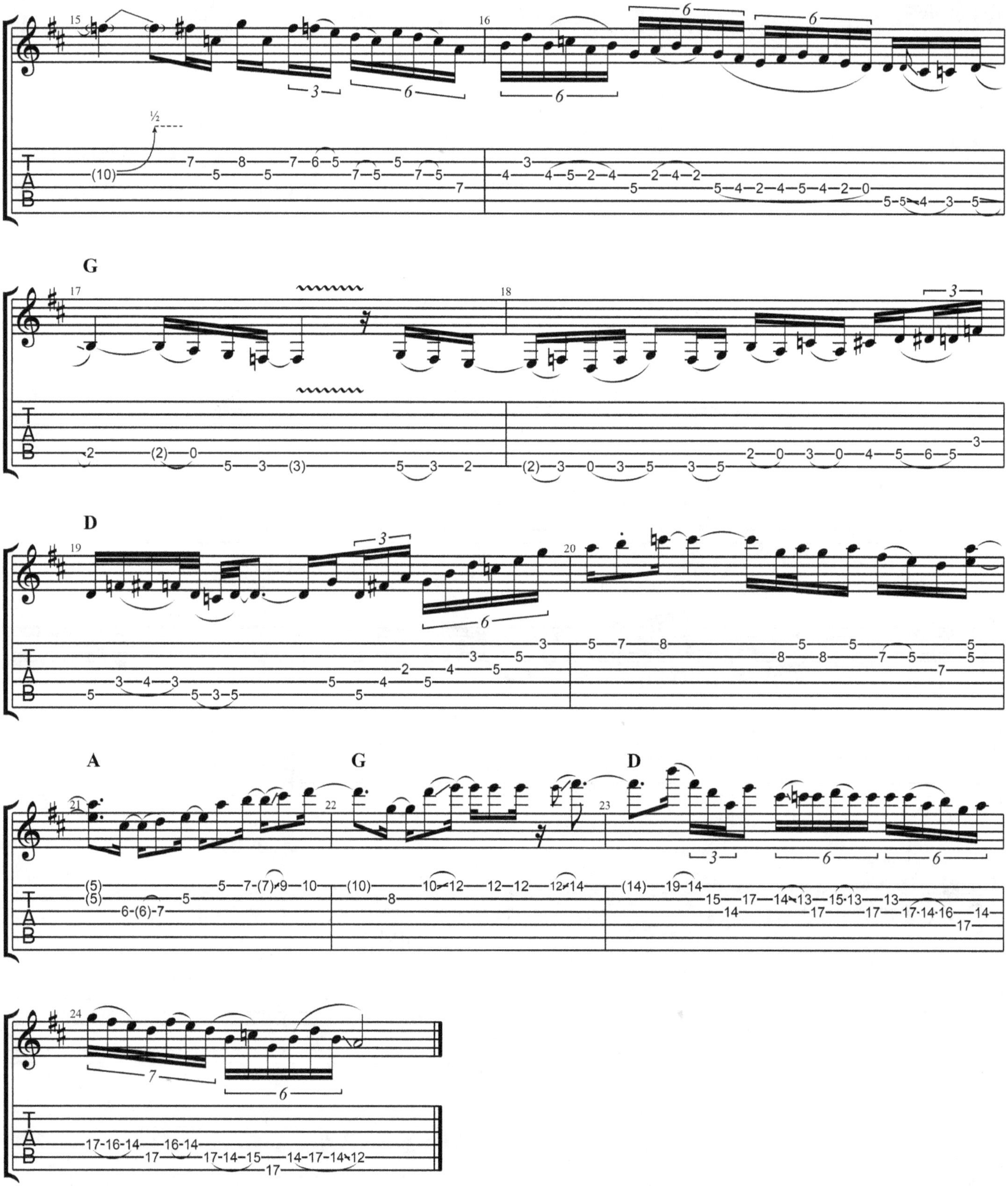
G
D
A
G
D

Chapter Five – Fusion Blues Vamp Soloing

Fusion is a genre of music that really loves a vamp – more so than other genres – so if you're going to play this type of music, it's good to be equipped with some creative ideas. In some respects, it's easier to come up with melodic ideas when faced with lots of chord changes, because the music has a natural direction and movement. But when the music is vamping on one chord, we need to be much more inventive and creative with our ideas.

In this chapter, we're going to look at ideas you can use over a ii V vamp in the key of G Major (Am7 to D7) and I'll demonstrate some of my Mixolydian vocabulary. In order to give purpose and direction to a progression that just loops around, we'll need to think carefully about phrasing and adding in some rhythmic surprises.

I'm using the D Mixolydian scale in these examples, which has the notes D E F# G A B C (like playing a G Major scale from D to D) and the examples are notated in the key of G Major, viewing D7 as the V chord.

This first example begins with a Mixolydian scale run before a slow bend up to the natural 6th of the Am chord. Highlighting important chord tones of the D9 (5th and 3rd) in bar two is a great way of signaling the change from Am to D9.

Example 5a

Next is a short two-bar lick featuring a call and response type phrase. In bar one, the first half of the line is the call and the response is played down an octave in the same bar. This phrase is developed in bar two. Call and response is an easy way to begin developing some vocal-like phrasing.

Example 5b

This line begins with a rapidly ascending 1/16th note run using a D Mixolydian scale sequence. By contrast, I take a quite different approach in bar two, using diatonic intervals drawn from the same scale, now played over the D9 chord. Sequencing intervals like this can really add a lot of melodic variety to a solo, rather than just playing the scale from one scale step to the next.

Example 5c

Here's a longer melodic idea that features plenty of legato phrasing. Notice how this line develops rhythmically, from bursts of 1/16th notes in bars 1-2 to the long passages beginning in bar three. Although the lick mostly employs 1/16th note variations, listen carefully to how the seven-note grouping is played in bar five on the final beat. Refer to the audio to get the exact rhythm used here.

Example 5d

Here is another D Mixolydian 1/16th note lick. In bar two, I introduce some chromatic notes to create tension. This is an idea often used in fusion to avoid playing predictable ideas. The use of off beat rhythms also helps to break up the construction of the phrase.

Example 5e

Example 5f uses the idea of superimposing other triads onto the D9 chord. At the end of bar two, a D minor, G minor and C major triad sequence is played over D9.

The idea here is that each triad has notes in common with the D9, but also contains extended or altered notes. Superimposing a C major triad over D9, for instance, creates the sound of a D11 chord. (The C, E and G of C major are the b7, 9th and 11th against a D dominant chord). Using triad combinations like this can really spice up a solo and give you good melodic contrast alongside scale passages.

Example 5f

Here is another line that uses the multiple triad approach – this time, A minor, D minor and G major over the D9 chord. The line finishes with three scale tones from D Mixolydian ending on the 4th/11th degree.

Example 5g

Example 5h is reminiscent of another of my influences, Larry Carlton, and uses a repeated sequence played on the top two strings. Phrases like this are a great way to develop your rhythmic vocabulary in soloing. Watch out for the 1/4 step bends as they are integral to the overall sound of the lick.

66

Example 5h

Rhythmic contrast is a simple way to keep things interesting in a solo. Bar one of this example is sparse, with long note durations, set against bar two's mostly 1/16th note scale sequence.

Example 5i

Here is another interval-driven line reminiscent of the kind of ideas Eric Johnson often plays. In a two-chord vamp situation like this, it's a highly effective device. Often, I will abandon the pick for this type of line and play it using the thumb and first finger. Alternatively, I'll hybrid pick, gripping the pick between the thumb and first finger, and using the second finger to pluck upwards.

Example 5j

The off beat rhythms in this line really bring the phrase to life and provide effective contrast to the longer legato lines of the previous examples.

Example 5k

This four-bar line demonstrates how effective position changes to different string sets can be in building an engaging solo. The lick builds from 5th position in bar one and gradually works its way up to 9th/10th position. Repetition of a phrase can also be used to great effect in fusion soloing, as in bar two.

Example 5l

Example 5m is another D Mixolydian scalic idea but adds some chromatic passing notes in bar two and concludes with some large intervals, employing the open second string for the surprise factor.

Example 5m

Here's a similar idea, with passing notes added to D Mixolydian in bar one. The entire line is played on the top three strings and the jump to the high A note on the first string 17th fret has a B.B. King blues quality to it. Moving quickly up or down in register like this can add some drama to a solo and helps to punctuate a melodic phrase.

Example 5n

In contrast to the scale run ideas, here's a line based on longer note durations and vocal-like bends.

Example 5o

In Example 5p, the open first string (the 6th degree of the G Major parent scale) creates a drone-type effect. In bar two, I'm using legato slides to enhance what would otherwise be a straightforward scale passage.

Example 5p

Finally, this line combines several legato ideas seen in previous licks. Bars 2-3 have Country-style hammer-ons and pull-offs to open strings, before a 1/16th note triplet legato run in bar four.

When working on these phrases, isolate any difficult passages and slow things down, committing the fingering to muscle memory.

Example 5q

Chapter Six – Bringing it All Together

In this final chapter we're going to further refine all the techniques and melodic ideas we've looked at in a fusion solo. This tune is essentially a minor blues, but it has a couple of harmonic twists added. Let's start by looking at the harmony of the tune.

Overview of the chord changes

We're in the key of G Minor and the first four bars follow a standard minor blues format. The vamp moves between Gm11 and Am11 and has a modal vibe.

| Gm11 Am11 | % | % | % |

When we move to the IV chord in bars 5-6, we'd normally expect to see two bars of C minor, but the harmony is spiced up with the addition of a substitution.

| Cm9 | B7#9 B7/F# |

A common way of playing these bars would be Cm7 – F7, resolving back to Gm7 – all chords from the parent key of G Minor. Instead, in bar six we have the b5 of F7. After playing the B7#9, a straight B7 chord is played, but voiced with its 5th (F#) in the bass, which creates a nice half step resolution to G minor.

As with a standard blues, we then return to the I chord for two bars.

| Gm11 Am11 | Gm11 |

Next comes the V chord and another harmonic twist in bars 9-10.

| D9 | Ebmaj9 Abmaj9 |

The substitution idea in bar 10 is based on a common movement you'll hear all the time in a standard blues setting: moving the V chord up and then back a half step. It's a simple way of creating a brief tension that soloists can take advantage of.

That movement would normally be played D9 – Eb9 – D9. Here, however, the quality of the Eb chord has been changed to an Ebmaj9. Having played that chord, it then made sense to use a "circle of fifths" idea and move to an Abmaj9 chord, which resolves nicely by a half step movement to Gm11.

We could have played one chord per beat here and continued the circle of fifths idea to have: Ebmaj9 – Abmaj9 – Dbmaj9 – Gbmaj9, resolving a half step up to Gm11. It's a way of bringing that Coltrane tonality into the blues.

In bars 11-12 the harmony ends as expected for a normal minor blues.

| Gm11 Am11 | Gm11 D9 |

At this point in the tune there is a bridging section. It's a complete departure from the blues format and is a game of two halves. First, we have four bars that are essentially a G minor vamp but played over a descending bassline.

| Gm Gm/F | Em7b5 Ebmaj7 |

| Gm Gm/F | Em7b5 Ebmaj7 |

This could have been written Gm, Gm/F, Gm/E, Gm/Eb, but since the final two chords are played using common Em7b5 and Ebmaj7 chord shapes, it made sense to indicate that in the notation. The sound achieved is exactly the same.

The next four-bar section is another departure from the G Minor blues harmony and also provides a way to lead back to it.

| Abmaj7 | Bmaj7 | Am7b5 D7alt |

First, we're back to the circle of fifths idea. We have just played an Ebmaj7 chord, so we can follow that with an Abmaj7.

Then comes a common idea in jazz harmony: to shift things around in minor 3rd internals (a distance of three frets). By "things" I mean chords, but it can also apply to melodic phrases. It's a device found in modern jazz used to create tension, or that "outside-inside" sound. It can be an exciting idea to play with, and if you keep on shifting upward in minor thirds, eventually you'll arrive back at the chord you started with!

We need a way of getting back to Gm11 though, and that is achieved via a simple minor ii V i movement: Am7b5 – D7alt – Gm11.

Everything we've covered so far is repeated, then the tune ends with a vamp that moves between G and F power chords.

Now that we have a handle on the harmony we're playing over, let's move on to an analysis of the ideas used in the solo. We'll break this down in two groups: *scale choices* and *melodic techniques*.

Solo Breakdown

Scale Choices

First, let's look at the scale ideas I applied throughout the solo. Because it's a G Minor blues, two tools that are of immediate use are the G Minor Pentatonic and G Blues scales. These will work perfectly well for most of the tune. Because of the modal feel of the piece, however, I also wanted to bring in the G Dorian scale for the more reflective/melancholy sound it offers.

I don't tend to see these scales as three distinct choices that I'm moving between. Instead, I prefer to think in terms of a hybrid G Minor scale that encompasses all three sounds.

If we combine the notes of the G Minor Pentatonic, G Blues and G Dorian scales we get a single eight-note hybrid scale comprising these notes:

G A Bb C Db D E F

Another way of looking at this is that it's a G Dorian scale with an added b5 (Db) tension note. Here's how the scale looks, arranged around a 3rd position box shape.

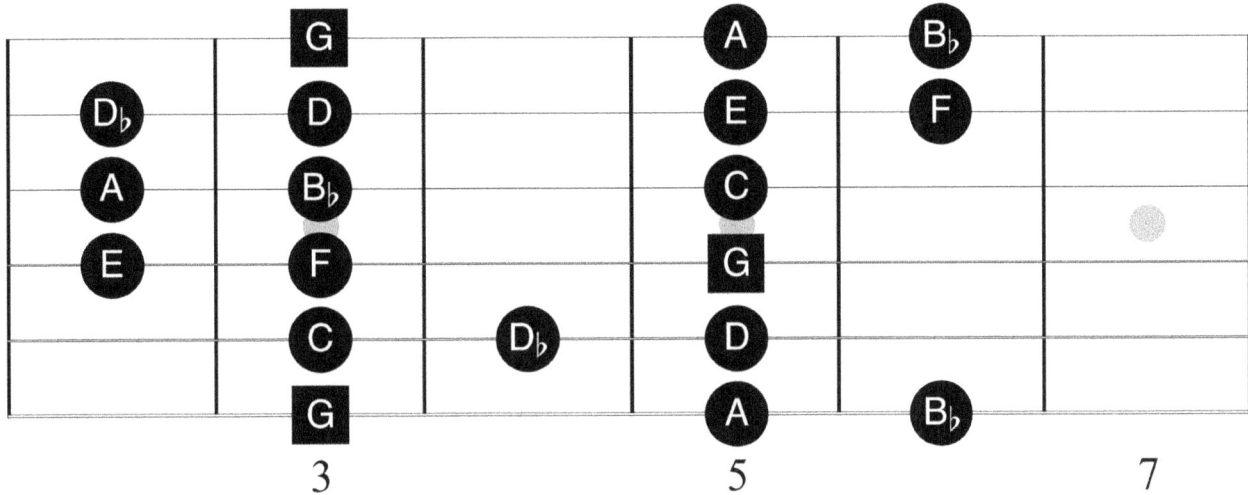

When soloing, I think of this hybrid scale providing my main notes choices, with pentatonic and blues ideas locked inside it that I can use when appropriate. I may also add further chromatic notes to this pattern if, for instance, I'm playing an ascending/descending run and want to have a repeating pattern of notes on each string.

As well as the b5 sound, when played over a straight Gm chord, the hybrid scale also contains notes that create an extended sound. The E note is the 6th/13th, the A is the 9th and the C is the 11th. Bars 2-3 of the solo are a good example of where I choose to highlight those extensions.

Example 6a

To deal with the dominant chords in this tune, I generally use two strategies.

Back in Chapter One I said there are three essential scales you need to know – Ionian (Major), Dorian (Minor) and Mixolydian (Dominant) – where we will spend the majority of our time when soloing. The first strategy then, is to play Mixolydian ideas over straight dominant 7 or 9 chords, such as in bar nine of the solo, where Gm11 transitions into D9.

Example 6b

The second strategy is a common jazz concept used to play over dominant chords with alterations. In bar six of the solo we have the first occurrence of B7#9. The B Altered scale is the perfect choice for soloing over this chord, as it contains all the tensions you can apply to a dominant chord (b5, #5, b9, #9). To save learning a new scale, however, jazz musicians often play a minor scale whose root is a half step above the dominant chord. i.e. over B7#9 we can play C minor ideas.

In this solo I used C Melodic Minor (C D Eb F G A B). When this scale is superimposed over a B7 chord it highlights the intervals shown in the table below. Notice it contains all four altered tensions, plus the root and b7 of the dominant chord.

C Melodic Minor	C	D	Eb	F	G	A	B
Intervals relative to B7	b9	#9	3rd (D#)	b5	#5	b7	Root

There is always an argument for learning scales from a root note, but the above approach is completely valid if you use your ears.

Example 6c

Melodic Techniques

Now that we know what scale choices fit the tune, creating a solo comes down to how we apply them. Below I have categorized the techniques I commonly use to tell a story with a solo and keep things from sounding routine or predictable. I use each of these devices multiple times during the solo, but I'll just highlight one instance of each melodic idea. Let's work through them.

Repeating rhythmic motifs

We spent an entire chapter looking at motifs as the source of melodic ideas. A motif can be a phrase that is moved through a scale, but also a repeating rhythmic idea as here in bars 31-32 of the solo.

Example 6d

Notes played in similar/identical patterns

In the previous idea, the rhythmic repetition used different notes, but it can also be the same notes that are repeated as in bars 33-34. Here, the motif repeats over the G minor chord but also spills over into bar thirty-four to be played briefly over the Em7b5.

Example 6e

Groups of 1/16th note triplets

I like the sound of 1/16th notes grouped in sixes for the rhythmic surprise it brings when played over a 4/4 groove. The solo actually begins with this idea in the pickup bar, but you'll find lots of examples of six-note groupings throughout.

Example 6f

Combinations of odd/even meter groupings

Once you get into the legato style of playing, it becomes easier to put together phrases that have unusual groupings of notes as you loop around hammer-on/pull-off patterns and allow them to "float" over the bar. This next example highlights bars 34-35 of the solo and is one of the most challenging runs in the piece. Learn this by playing it slowly. Work out an economical fingering first, then work on the timing and commit the whole thing to muscle memory.

Example 6g

Phrases that cross the bar line

One technique that can give a solo a real sense of continuity is playing phrases that cross the bar line. This stops a solo from sounding like a collection of licks strung together and adds flow. There are lots of examples of this throughout the solo, but here's this idea at work in bar 12-14.

Example 6h

All of the ideas so far have been to do with rhythmic phrasing. The final two ideas are to do with articulation.

Holdsworth-style legato phrases

Allan Holdsworth was a big influence on my playing and inspired my journey with legato playing. Here is a typical Allan-style ascending run that happens in bars 25-26.

Example 6i

Slurred approaches with hammer-ons and pull-offs

A technique I often use that comes from playing the blues is to slide into a target note from above or below. It's a simple idea but this articulation can inject your playing with a shot of soul that moves it from just playing notes to conveying an emotion. Slurring phrases also helps you to play a little behind the beat. Here's this idea used in bars 10-11 of the solo.

Example 6j

Now listen to the whole solo and hear all these ideas in context. Work through it in sections, breaking down any passages you find difficult and isolating those parts as smaller cells. Then have some fun jamming over the backing track.

Example 6k

Cm9
B7♯9
B7/F♯
Gm11
Am11
Gm11
D9
E♭maj9
A♭maj7
Gm11
Am11
Gm11
D9
Gm
Gm/F
Em7♭5
E♭maj7
full

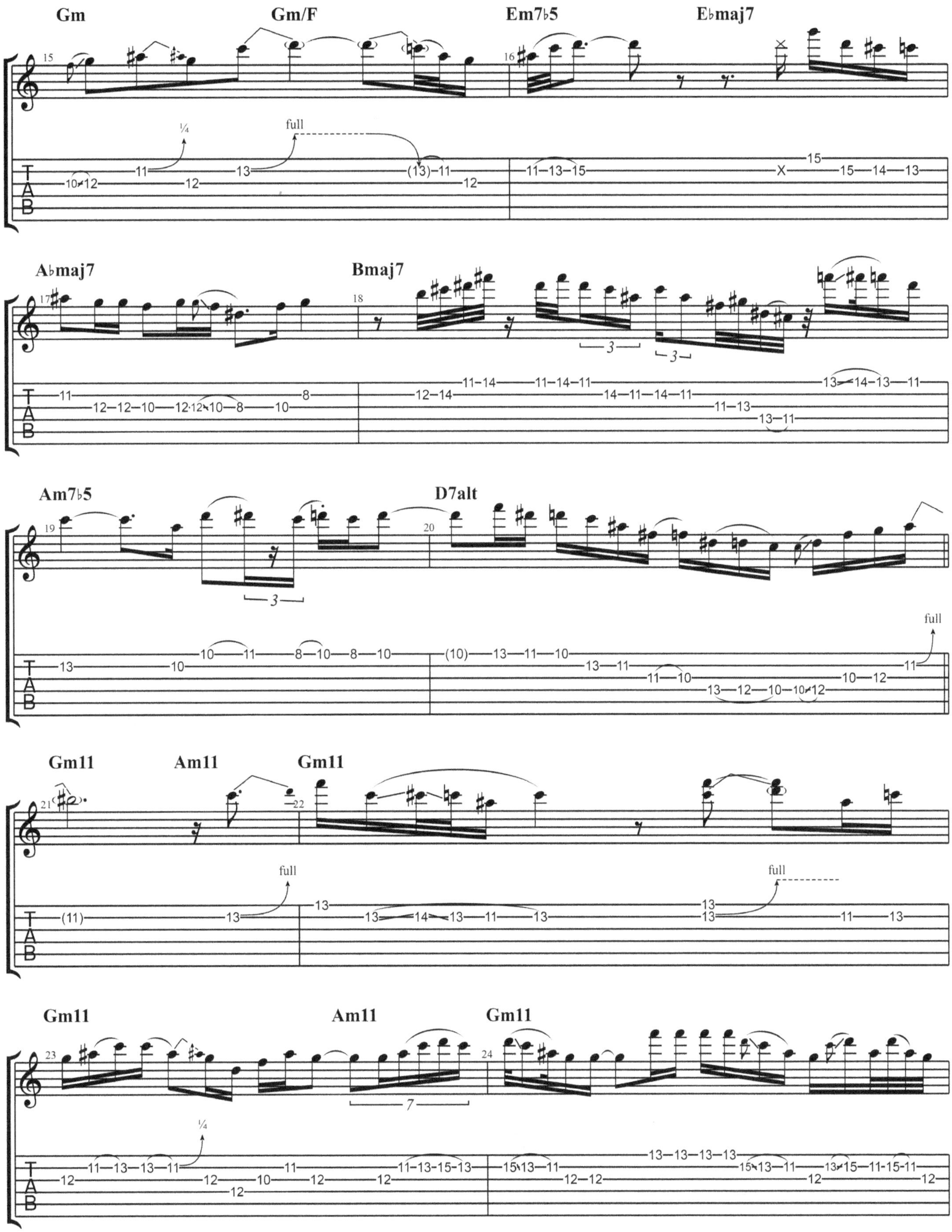
Gm
Gm/F
Em7♭5
E♭maj7
¼
full
A♭maj7
Bmaj7
Am7♭5
D7alt
full
Gm11
Am11
Gm11
full
full
Gm11
Am11
Gm11
¼

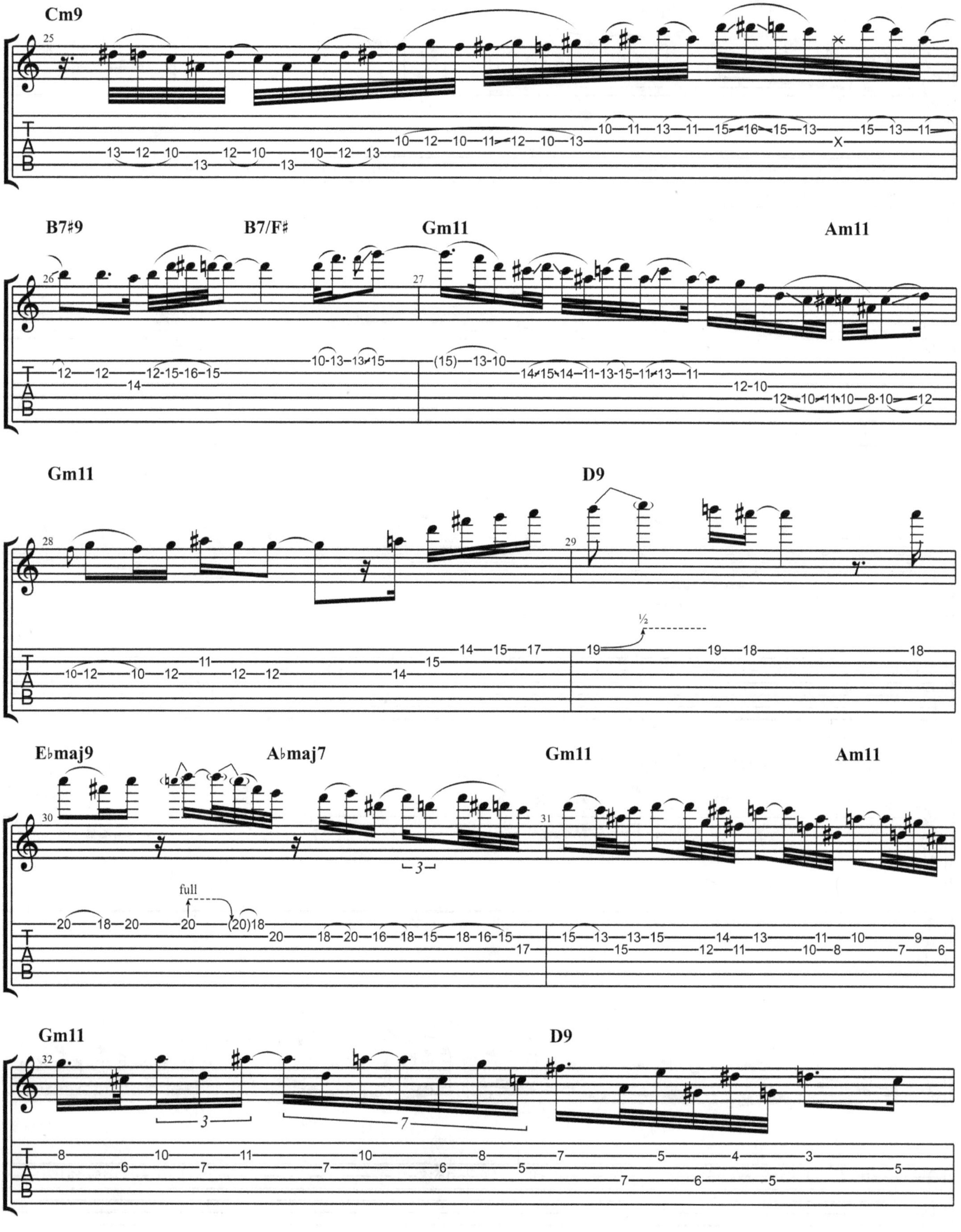
Cm9
B7♯9
B7/F♯
Gm11
Am11
Gm11
D9
½
E♭maj9
A♭maj7
Gm11
Am11
full
Gm11
D9

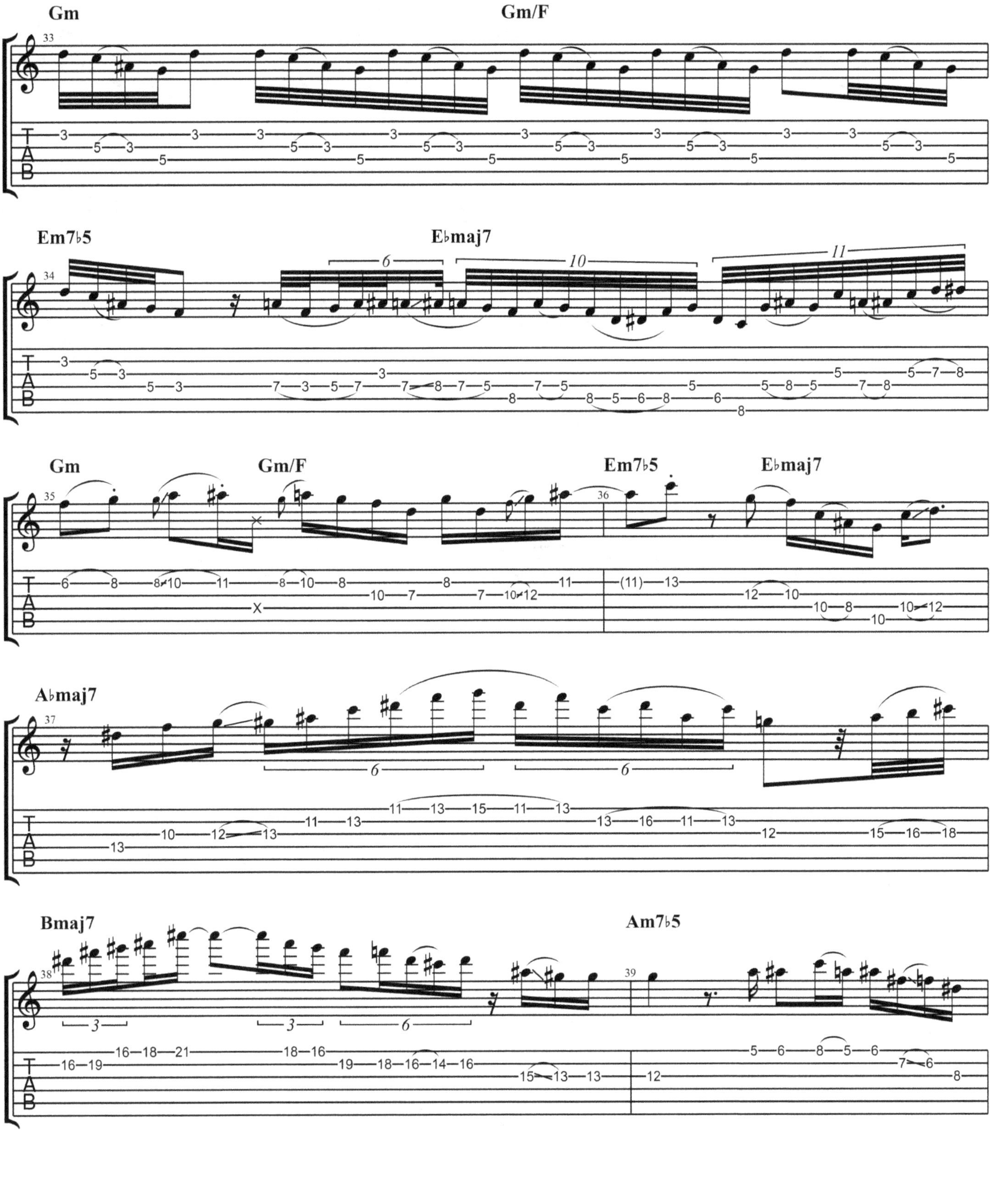
Gm
Gm/F
Em7♭5
E♭maj7
Gm
Gm/F
Em7♭5
E♭maj7
A♭maj7
Bmaj7
Am7♭5

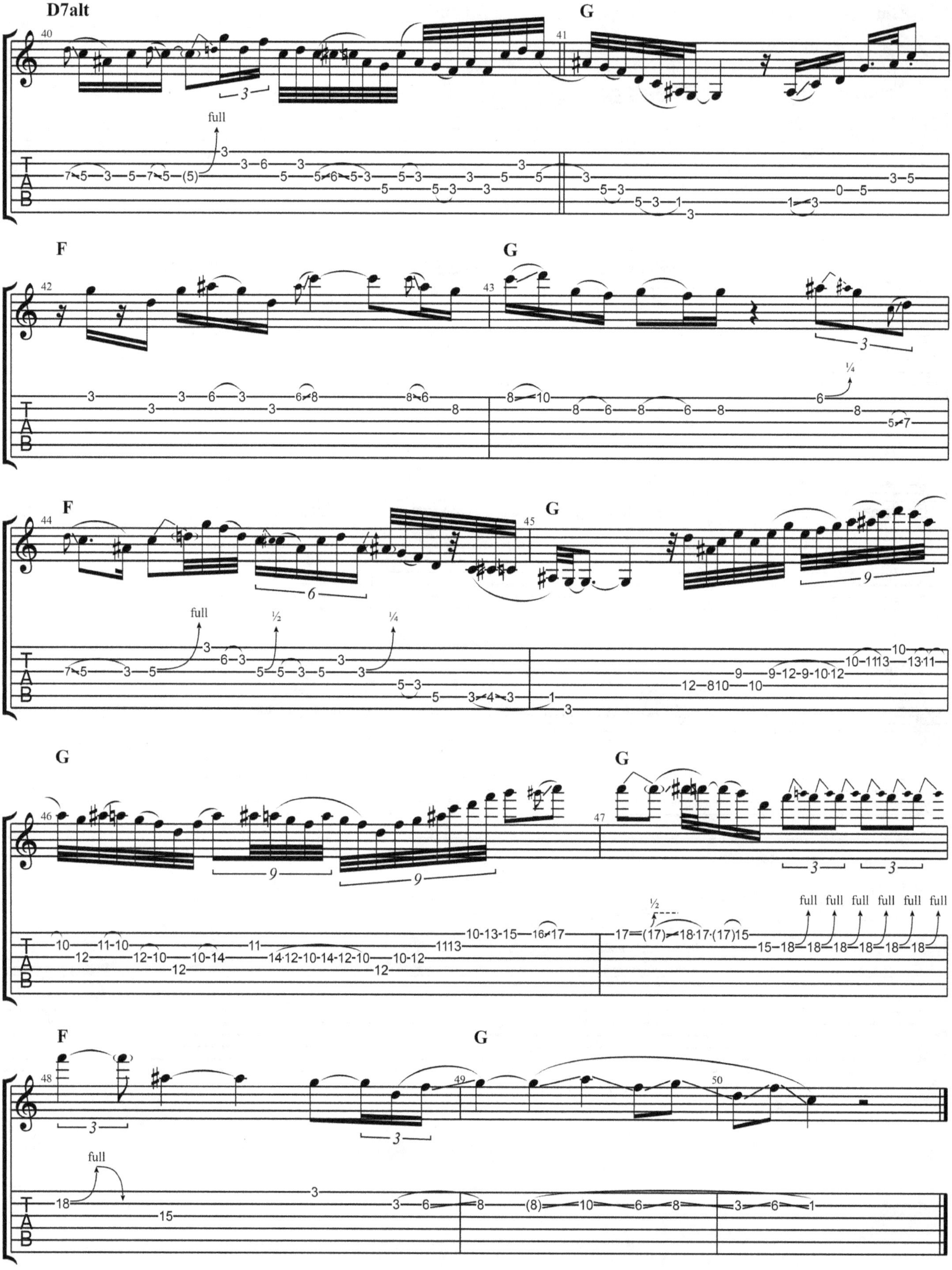
D7alt
G
F
G
F
G
G
G
F
G

Stay in Touch

To find out what I'm doing currently, stop by my website at:

https://www.allenhinds.com

You can also connect with me on Facebook:

https://www.facebook.com/allenhindsguitarist/

And Instagram:

https://www.instagram.com/hindsybabe/

I'm currently giving one-to-one lessons via zoom. Find out more here:

https://www.allenhinds.com/online-lessons

www.ingramcontent.com/pod-product-compliance
Lightning Source LLC
Chambersburg PA
CBHW081437090426

42740CB00017B/3337